How to Draw Graffiti Art (This How to Draw Graffiti Book Contains Examples of Graffiti Letters, Graffiti Names and Graffiti Drawings)

This book includes ideas on how to draw graffiti art step by step and in total shows how to draw 30 different graffiti tags

James Manning

How to Draw Graffiti Art

Introduction

Drawing stimulates parts of the brain that are responsible for creative thinking and imagination. From a young age, we are all creatively encouraged to draw, often to improve our fine motor skills and co-ordination.

From toddler 'scribbles' to 'matchstick men' you may find that as you get older you will want to tackle more complex drawings (perhaps it's an image you have seen in a book) but as you begin to put pencil to paper you may have no idea where to start, causing you frustration and annoyance.

With the help of our 'How to Draw' book series, this frustration will disappear as we guide you step by step, line by line, to create your very own masterpieces!

Each illustration in this book is deconstructed and simplified into lines and shapes that will not overwhelm you. As we guide you to form each simple line and shape together on the paper, the image gradually becomes more detailed and textured.

There will be such a sense of accomplishment and achievement once your drawing is complete, which in turn will boost your self-esteem and confidence.

Drawing Characters Step-by-Step

If at first, you find my step-by-step approach too complicated or difficult please leave it to one side and come back to it later. Instead, use the grids with numbers and letters on it first. By following the coordinates and matching them up with the coordinates on a blank grid you can redraw the characters that way instead.

What to do if you get frustrated whilst drawing

You may find that whilst working through my 'How to Draw' series, you may become frustrated as you find learning the new skill harder than you may have first anticipated. What you have drawn on the paper may be different to how you envisioned it to look, or you may be constantly comparing your skill to friends and siblings efforts. Learning a brand new skill can be difficult and time consuming, and you will need to remind yourself that everyone learns and works at different paces and that it is perfectly fine for you to take your time in refining your new skill.

If you find that your concentration is lost and you become agitated and frustrated with your work, it is very important to try and keep the activity fun and engaging, so encouraging regular breaks is imperative. It may even be better to encourage yourself to do a completely different activity for a while and come back to drawing tomorrow.

Validating your feelings is also crucial. It is okay for you to feel annoyed and frustrated, but always encourage yourself to keep trying. Perhaps tell yourself to take a step back in the book and repeat a part that you have already mastered, then gradually move onto the step that you are finding trickier.

Everyone, including adults and the most successful artists can make mistakes, and sometimes these mistakes could even be successes! The extra line or shape you may have drawn accidently, could become part of the drawing as a whole and copying the lines exactly as they are in the book isn't a necessity.

Try to always reinforce to yourself that the best way to learn when drawing is to learn from mistakes and continue on.

James Manning, ClinPsyD

HOW TO DRAW GRAFFITI ART

Here are all of the drawings in this book. I guess it must seem like there is a lot of them when they are looked at all at once!

Luckily, I am not going to ask you to draw them all straight away. The best way to learn to draw is one step at a time. Each drawing in this book may require between 50 and 200 strokes of your pencil, but all you will need to think about is drawing one stroke at a time.

As you use your pencil, stroke by stroke, working your way through this book, you will eventually be able to create all of the drawings!

Drawing Step-by-Step

In this book I will show you how to create 30 different drawings step by step. Each step will build on the previous one until eventually you have 30 complete drawings.

To make things easier for you, please download the outline grids for the drawings. You can download this additional book with all of them inside for free by visiting the web address below:

https://www.lipdf.com/product/graffitiart/

At first, you find my step-by-step approach too complicated or difficult please leave it to one side and come back to it later. Instead, you may want to use an alternative grid with numbers and letters on it first. By following the coordinates and matching them up with the coordinates on a blank grid you can redraw the pictures this way instead.

I have put details below about where you can download these basic grids for free on the internet.

https://www.lipdf.com/product/grids/

You can of course ask an adult to help you draw the grids instead, or you may even feel able to draw them yourself.

Please see page 40 for the webpage address for your bonus books and the password.

1. Although this is the first drawing in this book, you don't have to start drawing here! Flick through the book and find your favourite drawing to start with.

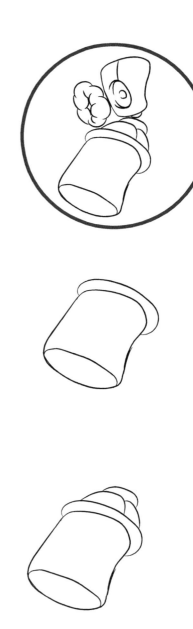

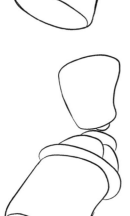

You can download blank grids to practice with in dark and light PDF formats by following the link below.

https://www.lipdf.com/product/grids/

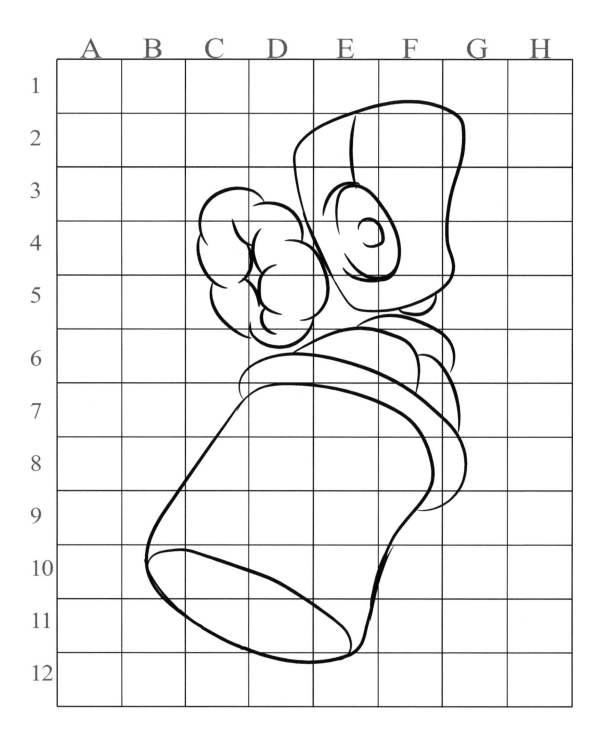

2. It's unlikely you will get everything right the first time. Draw in pencil so you can erase any mistakes.

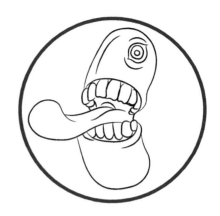

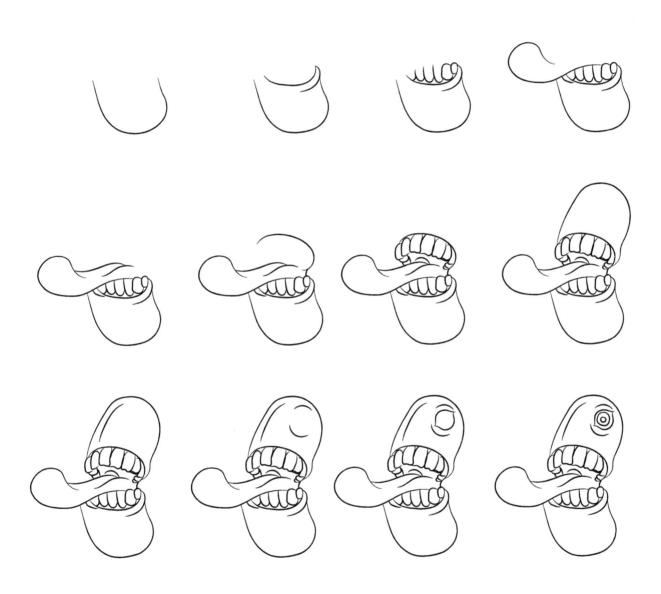

You can download blank grids to practice with in dark and light PDF formats by following the link below.

https://www.lipdf.com/product/grids/

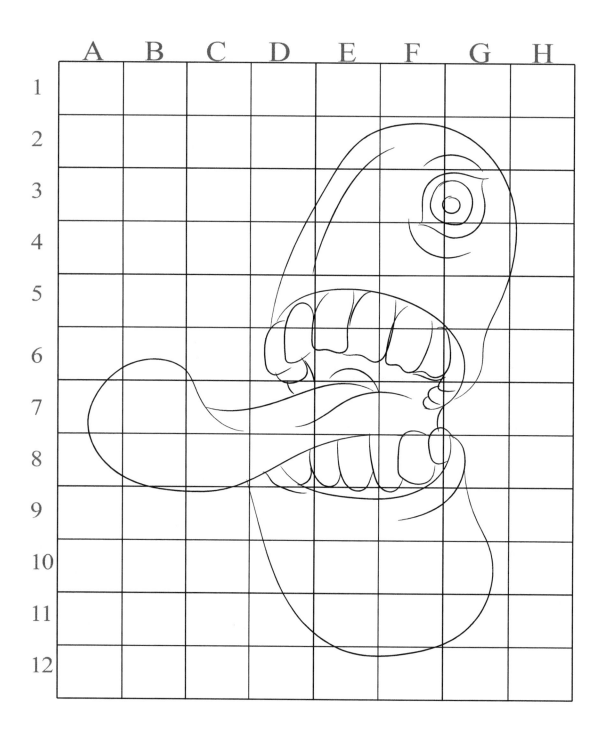

3. Why not experiment with how you hold your pencil? How you hold a pen for handwriting may not be comfortable for drawing.

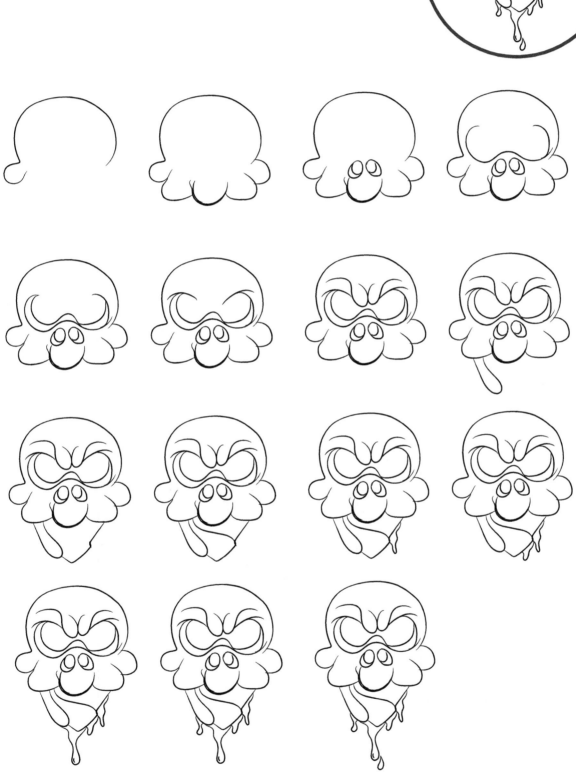

11

You can download blank grids to practice with in dark and light PDF formats by following the link below.

https://www.lipdf.com/product/grids/

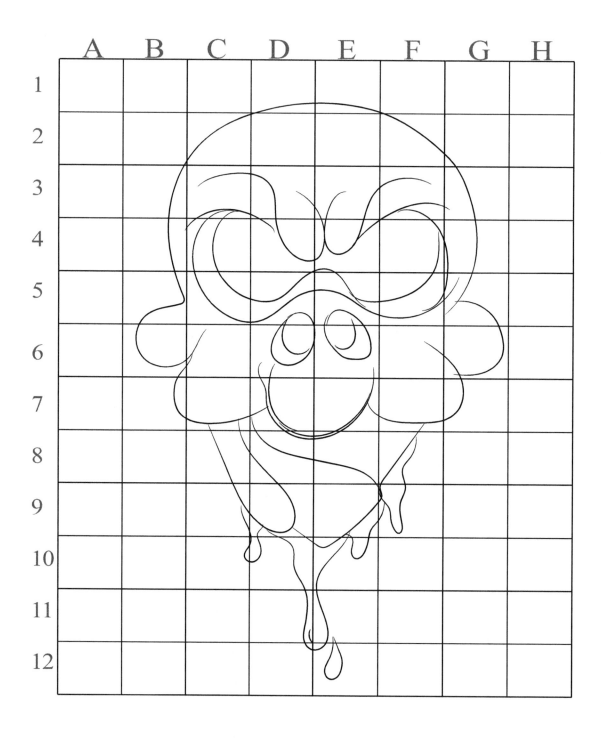

4. There are no rules with art. Feel free to interpret the drawing in your own style.

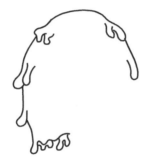

You can download blank grids to practice with in dark and light PDF formats by following the link below.

https://www.lipdf.com/product/grids/

5. Patience is key. If you are getting irritated with your work, leave it for now and come back to it later.

You can download blank grids to practice with in dark and light PDF formats by following the link below.

https://www.lipdf.com/product/grids/

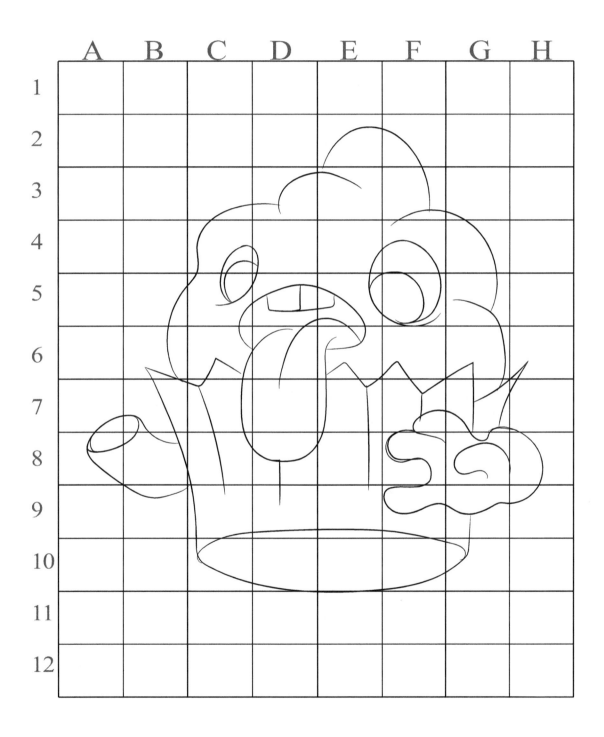

6. You could have a go at very roughly sketching out the shapes, then going over the lines in pen. Once finished, erase out the rough lines.

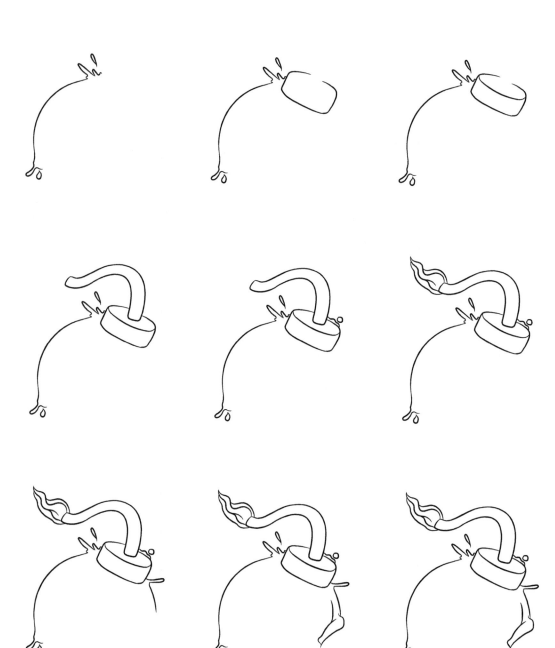

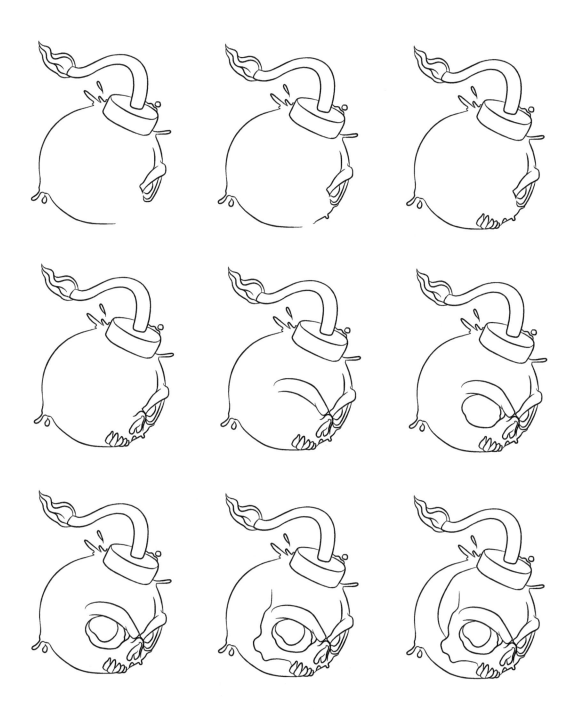

You can download blank grids to practice with in dark and light PDF formats by following the link below.

https://www.lipdf.com/product/grids/

7. If you struggle with this particular drawing, stop where you are and try another page in this book. You can always come back to this page later.

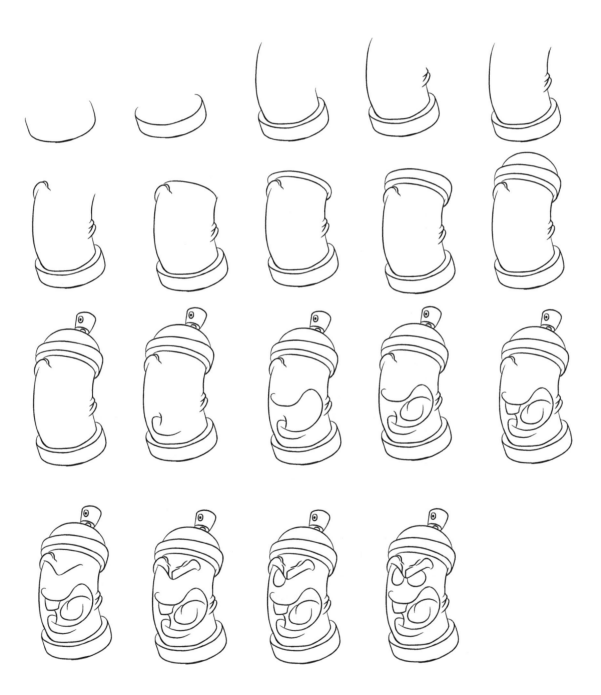

You can download blank grids to practice with in dark and light PDF formats by following the link below.

https://www.lipdf.com/product/grids/

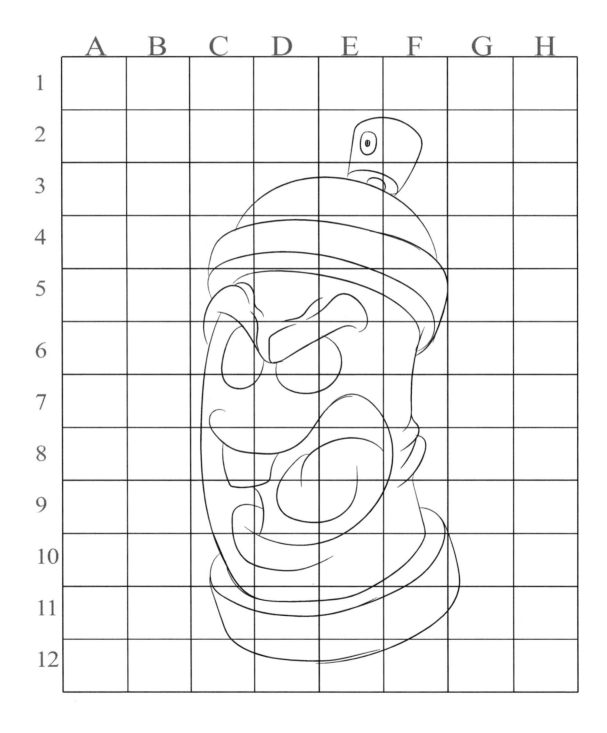

8. Drawing a little everyday will help your drawing improve, stick with it!

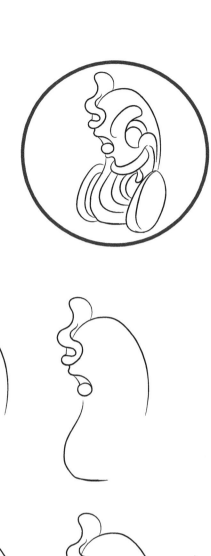

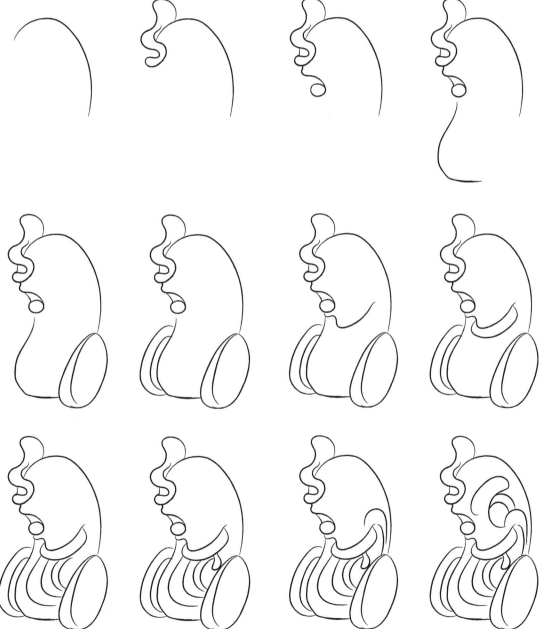

You can download blank grids to practice with in dark and light PDF formats by following the link below.

https://www.lipdf.com/product/grids/

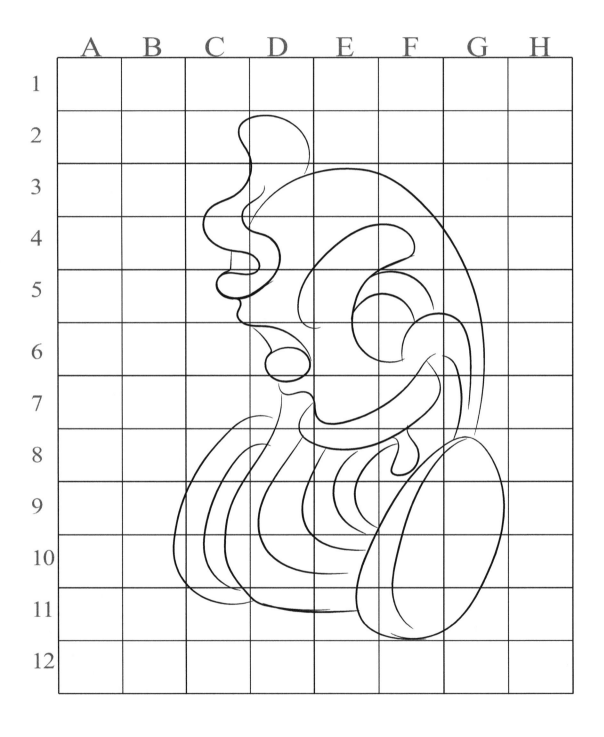

9. If you want to, you could practice different types of pencil strokes on a scrap piece of paper. What happens when you press hard with the pencil? What happens when you use the edge of the pencil rather than the point?

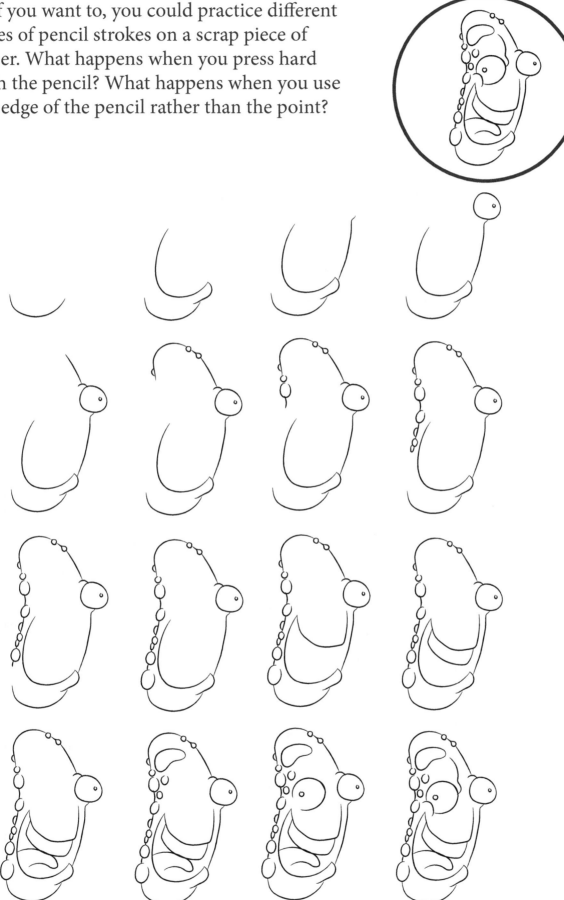

You can download blank grids to practice with in dark and light PDF formats by following the link below.

https://www.lipdf.com/product/grids/

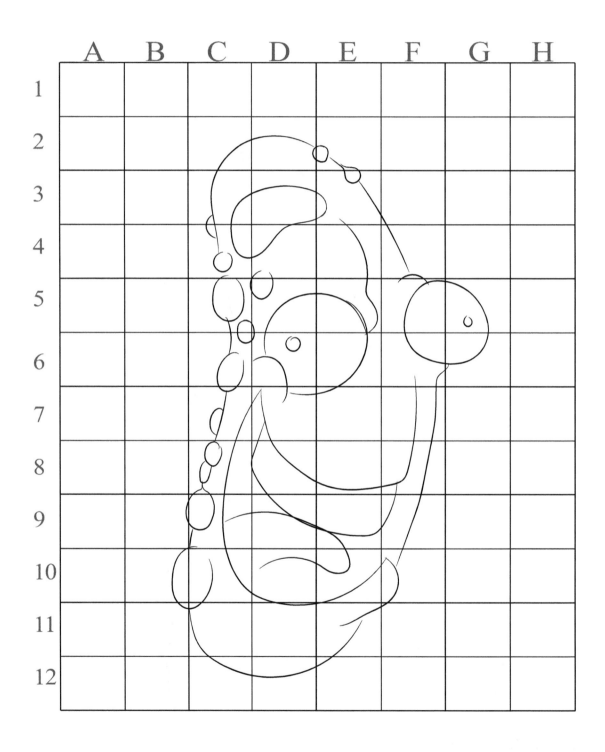

10. Always keep your hand relaxed, you will be surprised to see how your drawing flows on the paper when you aren't pressing too hard with the pencil.

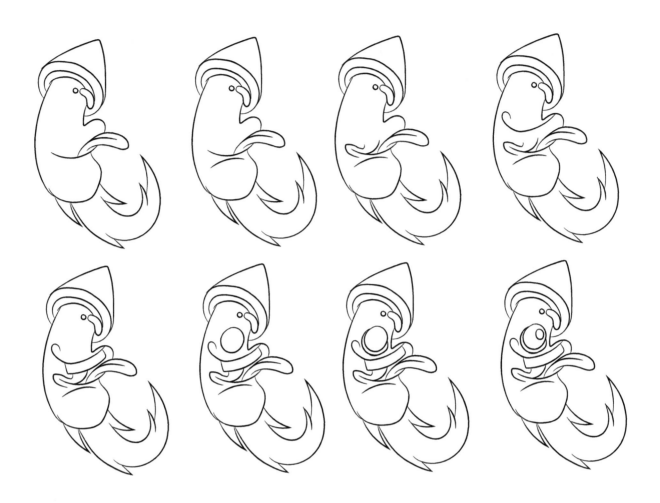

You can download blank grids to practice with in dark and light PDF formats by following the link below.

https://www.lipdf.com/product/grids/

11. Try out a "warm up" exercise before starting your drawing. Have a go at straight, curved and zig zag lines on a scrap piece of paper.

30

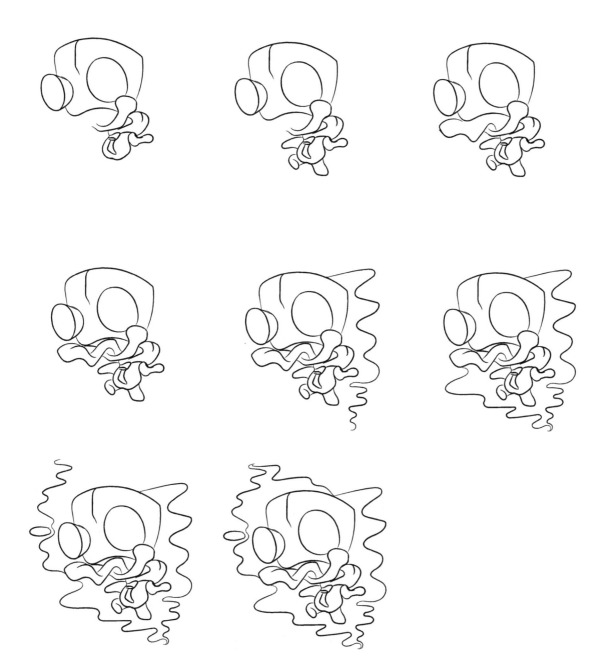

You can download blank grids to practice with in dark and light PDF formats by following the link below.

https://www.lipdf.com/product/grids/

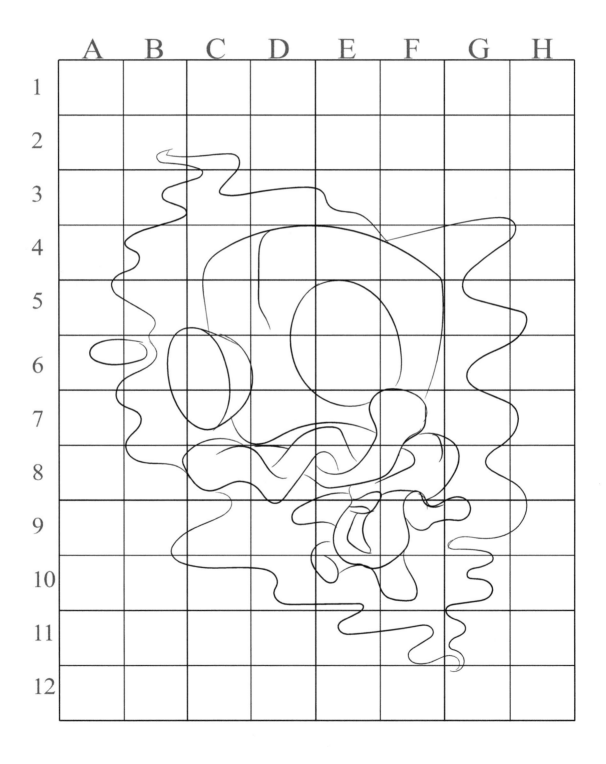

12. Try out doodling on a scrap piece of paper before starting this drawing, it will help with your concentration and creativity!

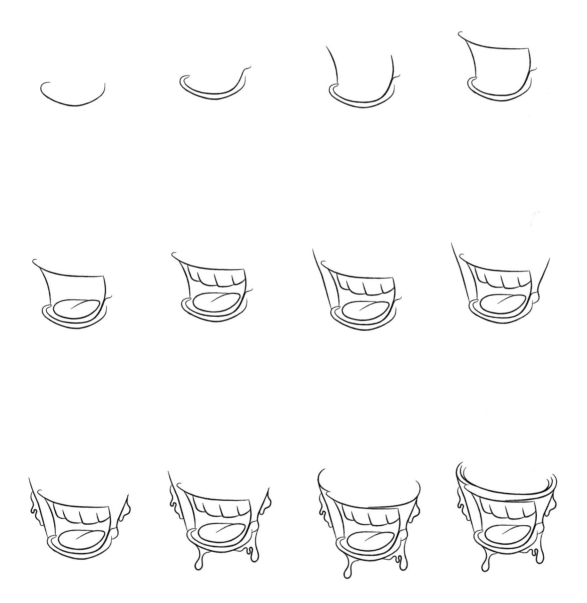

You can download blank grids to practice with in dark and light PDF formats by following the link below.

https://www.lipdf.com/product/grids/

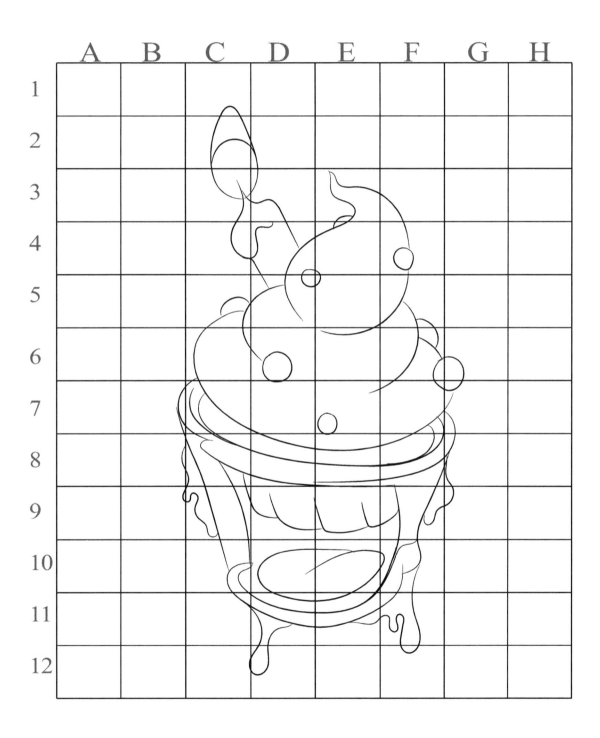

13. If you are struggling to draw a long line, try sketching much shorter lines joined together. You will find your pencil is much easier to control.

You can download blank grids to practice with in dark and light PDF formats by following the link below.

https://www.lipdf.com/product/grids/

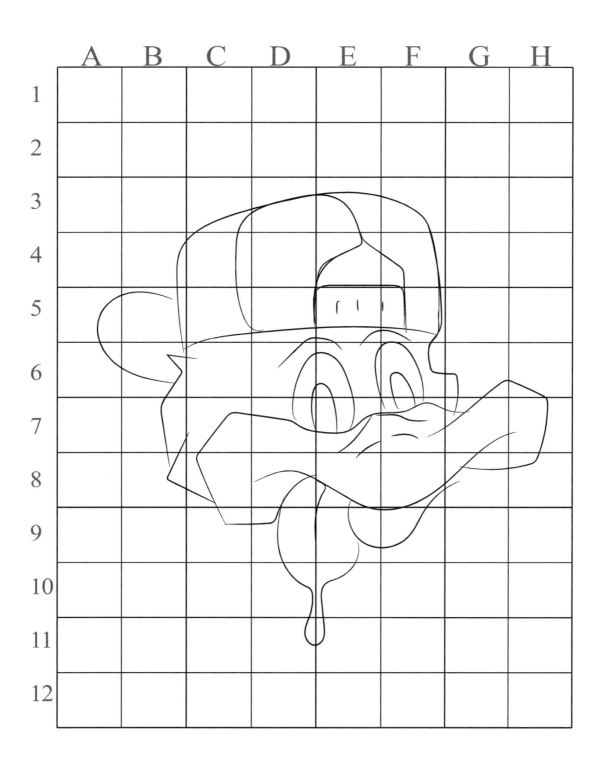

14. Stay creative! You don't have to copy the image exactly as I have laid it out, just use the lines as a guide.

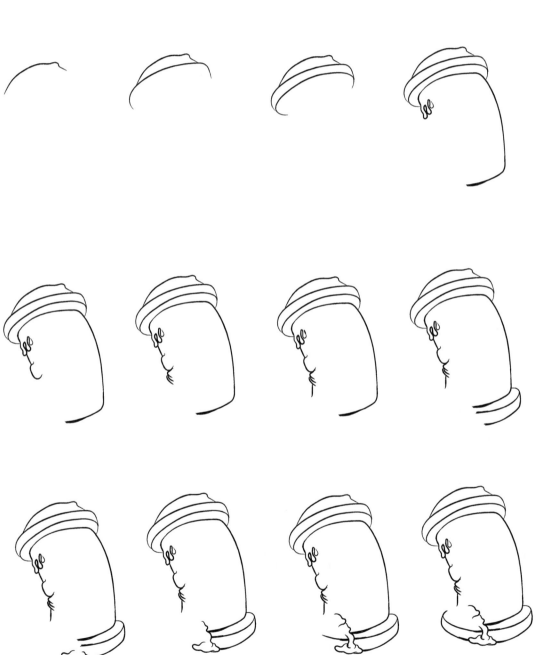

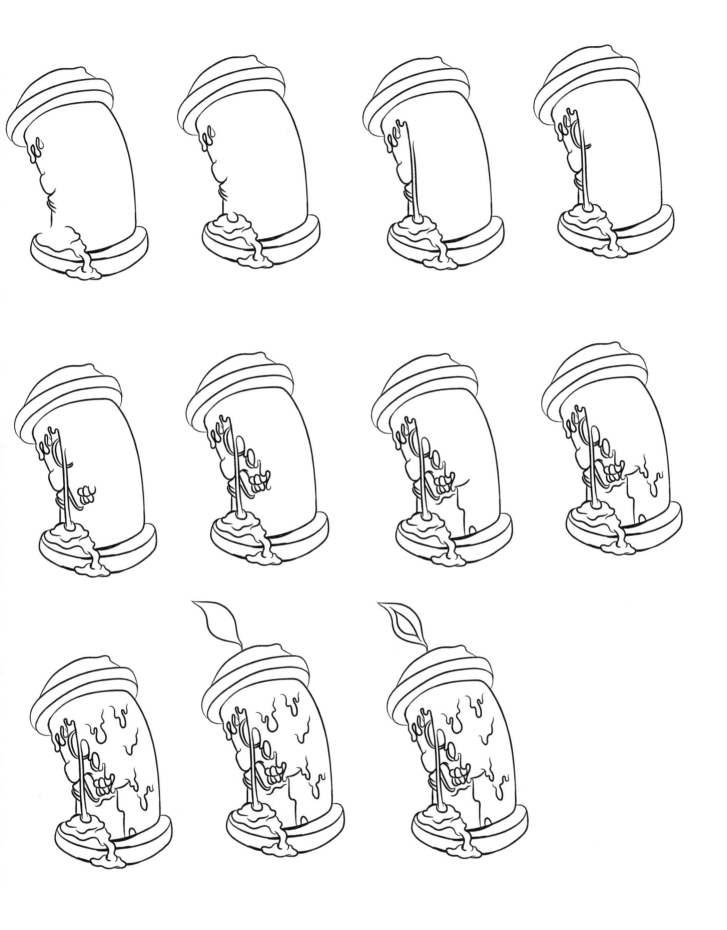

You can download blank grids to practice with in dark and light PDF formats by following the link below.

https://www.lipdf.com/product/grids/

https://www.lipdf.com/product/htdbooks/
Password: 6t5we3

15. Try not to get annoyed if what you've drawn on the paper isn't as you had envisioned, keep on going and you'll find that every pencil stroke will eventually come together.

You can download blank grids to practice with in dark and light PDF formats by following the link below.

https://www.lipdf.com/product/grids/

16. Remember to take regular breaks, this will help boost your concentration and prevent you from getting too tired.

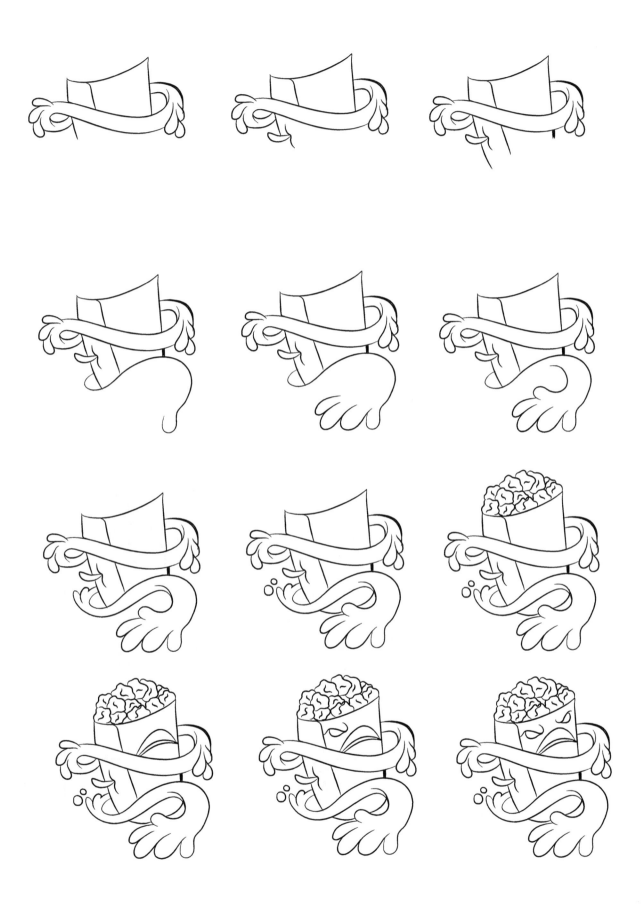

You can download blank grids to practice with in dark and light PDF formats by following the link below.

https://www.lipdf.com/product/grids/

17. If you are becoming frustrated and finding the next step of the drawing a challenge, keep yourself calm and go back a few steps. By repeating the last few steps you may find this helps you flow into the step you are finding difficult.

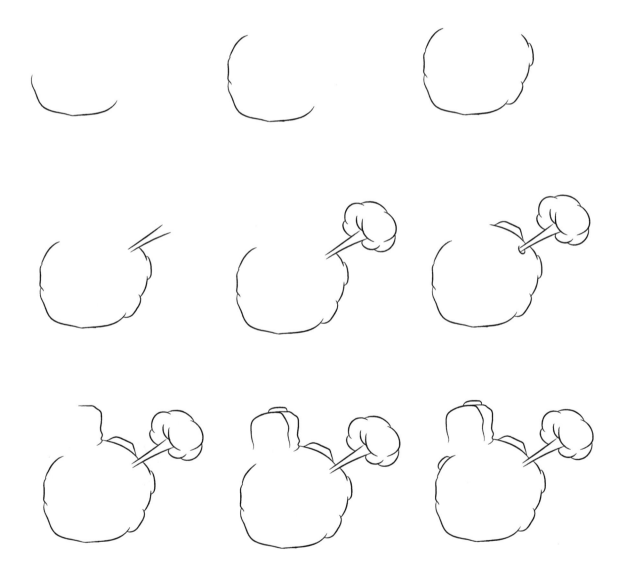

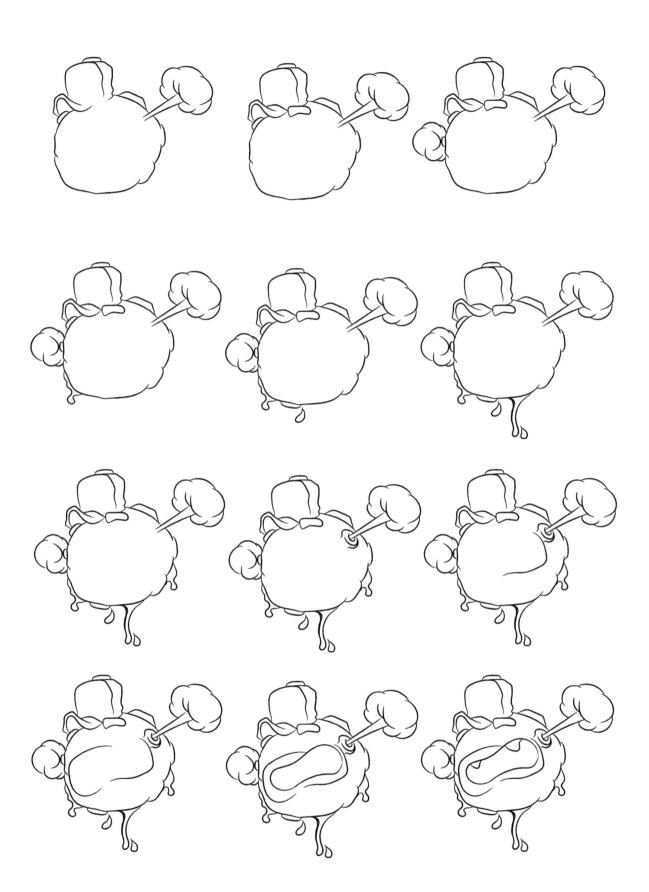

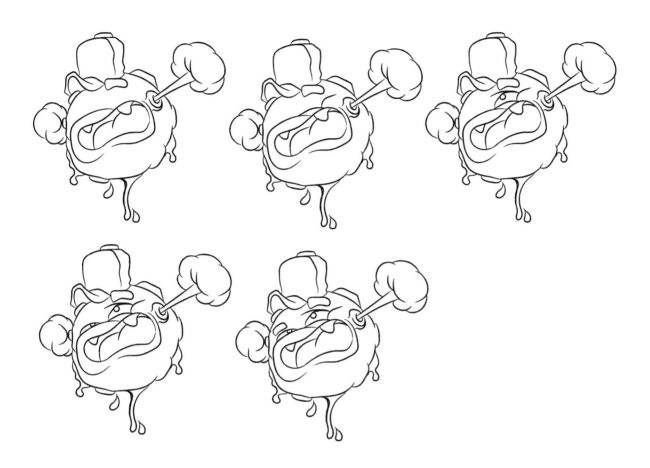

You can download blank grids to practice with in dark and light PDF formats by following the link below.

https://www.lipdf.com/product/grids/

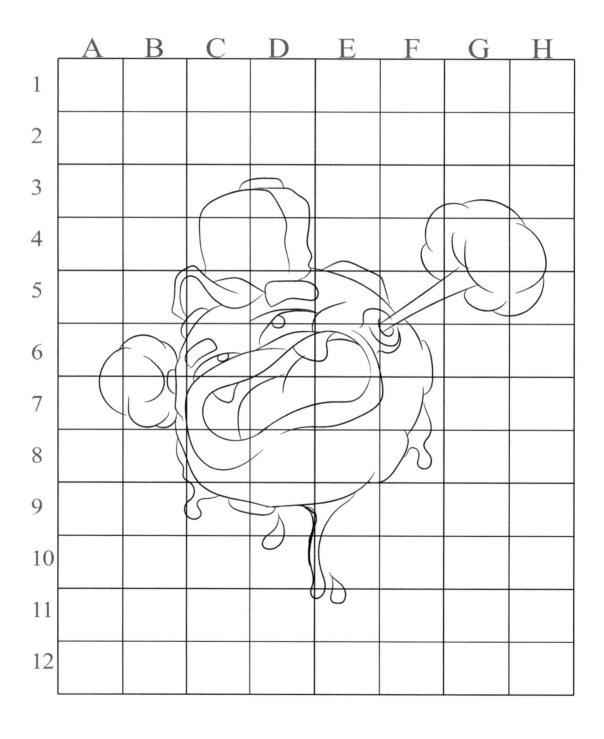

18. Art is all about interpretation and expression, so use the images as a guide and alter them to your own preferences.

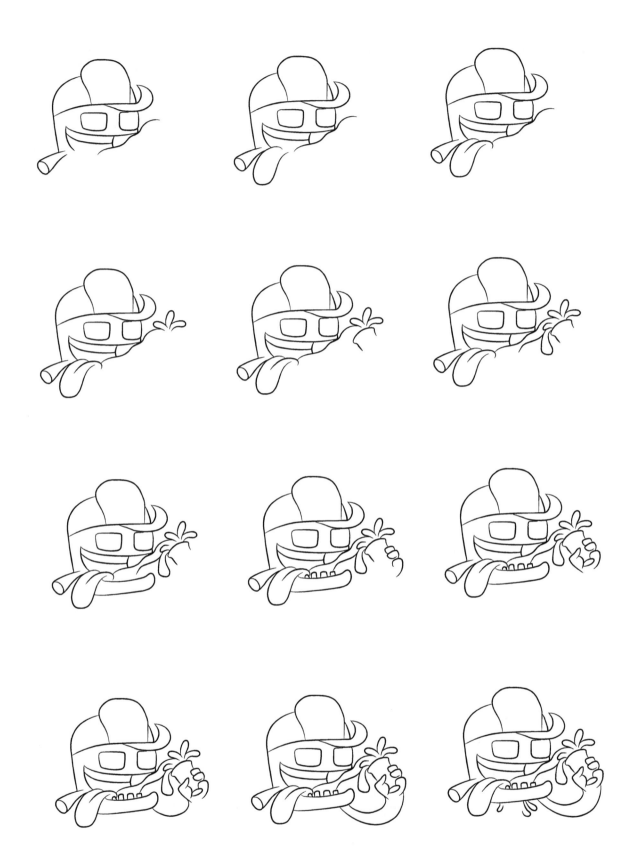

You can download blank grids to practice with in dark and light PDF formats by following the link below.

https://www.lipdf.com/product/grids/

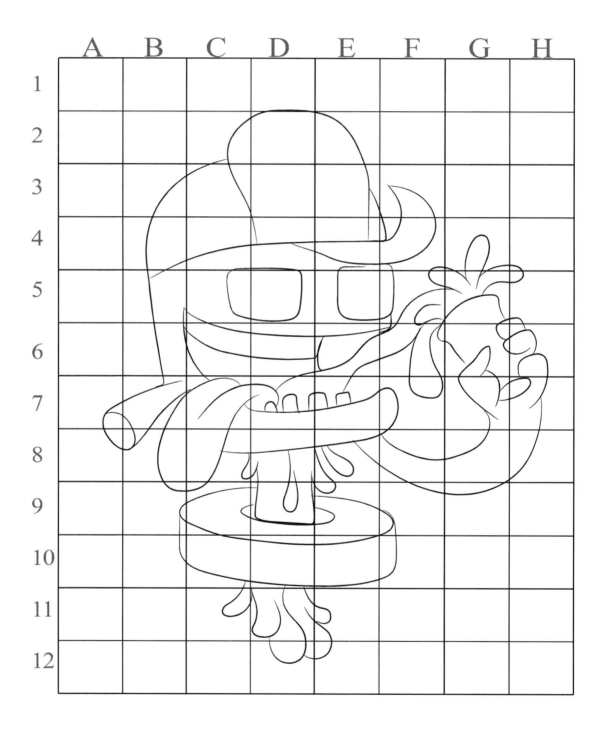

19. If you keep up with drawing every day, you will be surprised at the improvements you'll see in your sketches!

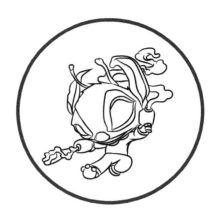

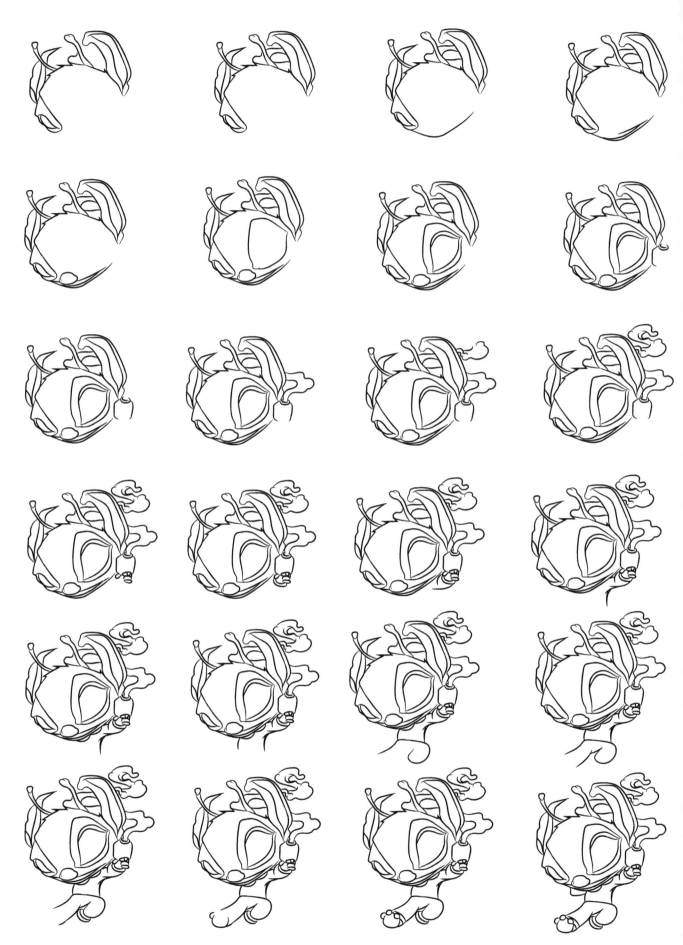

You can download blank grids to practice with in dark and light PDF formats by following the link below.

https://www.lipdf.com/product/grids/

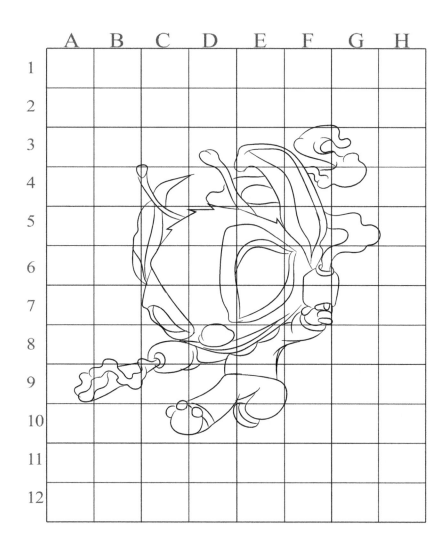

20. Begin by drawing a basic sketch drawn very lightly in pencil. This sketch will help you keep your drawing in perspective.

You can download blank grids to practice with in dark and light PDF formats by following the link below.

https://www.lipdf.com/product/grids/

21. Adding one section of your project at a time will make your drawing feel less overwhelming.

You can download blank grids to practice with in dark and light PDF formats by following the link below.

https://www.lipdf.com/product/grids/

22. Creativity does not necessarily involve logic. The brain is very good as solving pattern challenges if you give it a chance.

You can download blank grids to practice with in dark and light PDF formats by following the link below.

https://www.lipdf.com/product/grids/

23. Creativity does not necessarily involve logic. The brain is very good as solving pattern challenges if you give it a chance.

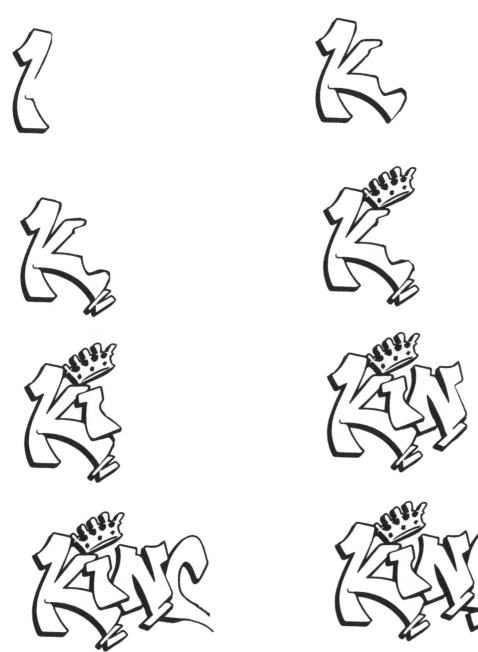

You can download blank grids to practice with in dark and light PDF formats by following the link below.

https://www.lipdf.com/product/grids/

24. To give your brain a workout, complete a drawing in an opposite way to way you would normally approach it. Sometimes this can help us see things that we did not notice before.

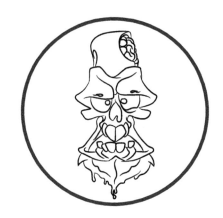

 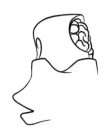  

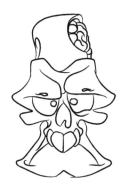

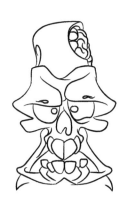

You can download blank grids to practice with in dark and light PDF formats by following the link below.

https://www.lipdf.com/product/grids/

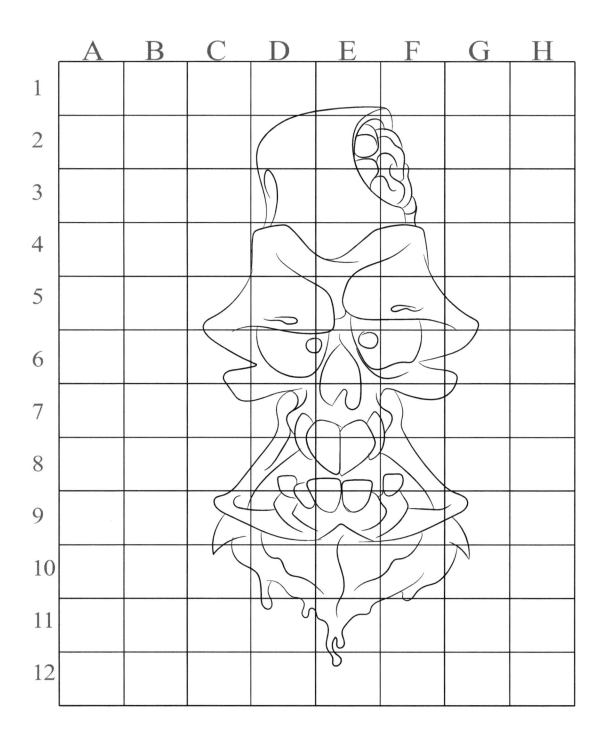

25. After you have sketched out this drawing step by step, add extra features to make it look more original or personal to you.

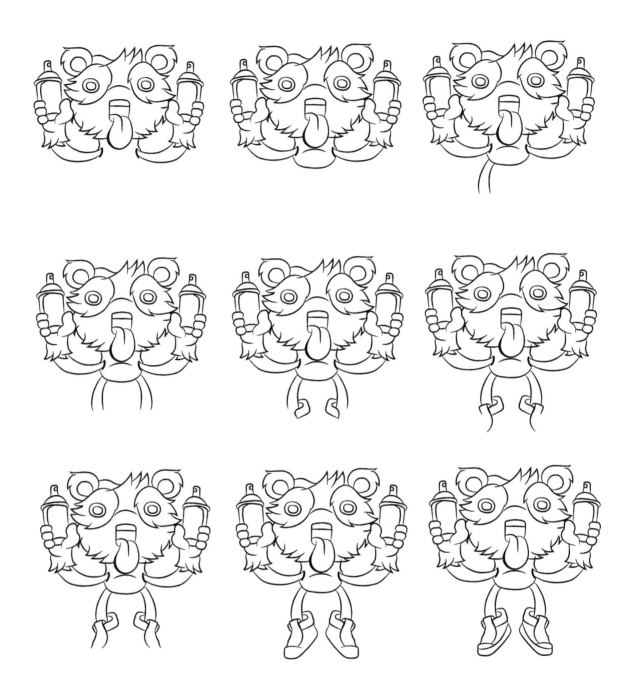

You can download blank grids to practice with in dark and light PDF formats by following the link below.

https://www.lipdf.com/product/grids/

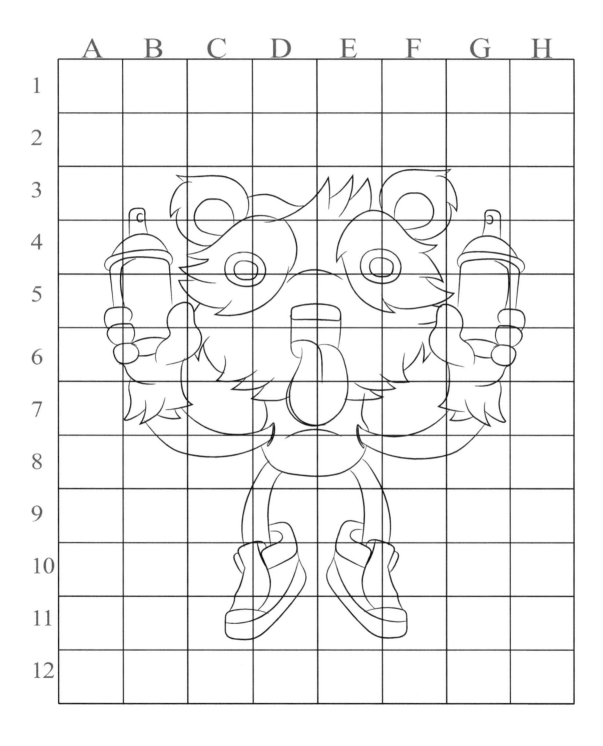

26. Ask questions to stimulate your creativity. Following this, listen to the suggestions your mind comes up with.

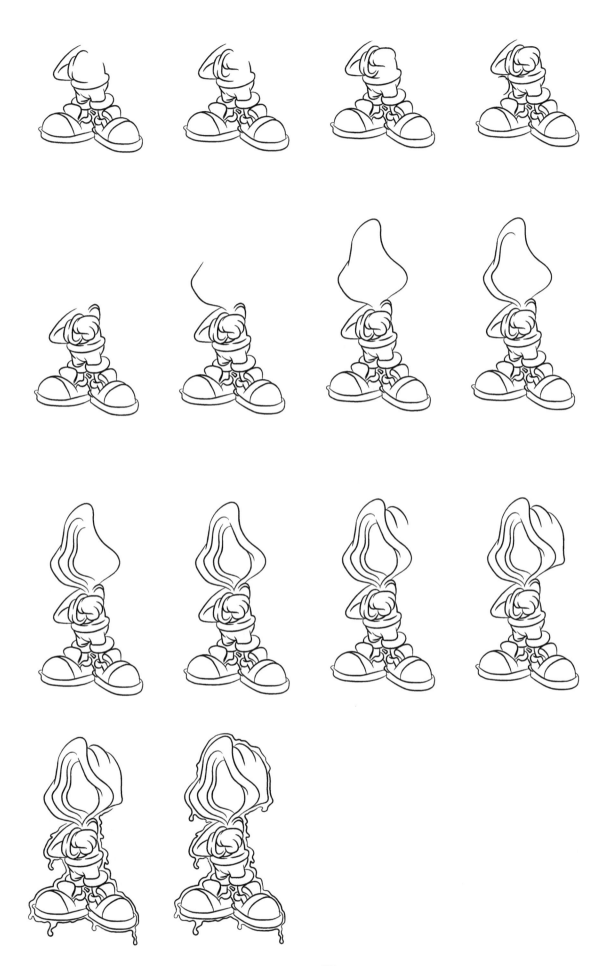

You can download blank grids to practice with in dark and light PDF formats by following the link below.

https://www.lipdf.com/product/grids/

27. This is one of the most complex drawings in this book. When starting a more complex drawing it is best to think of it as a lot of small parts. Focusing on one small part at a time will make your project feel less overwhelming.

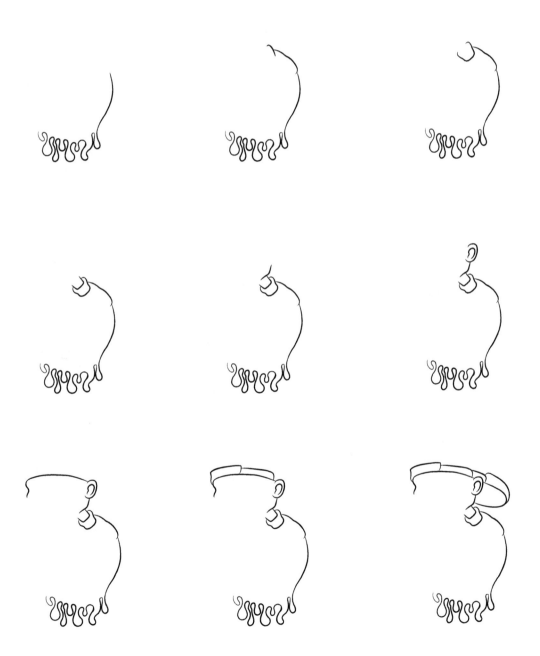

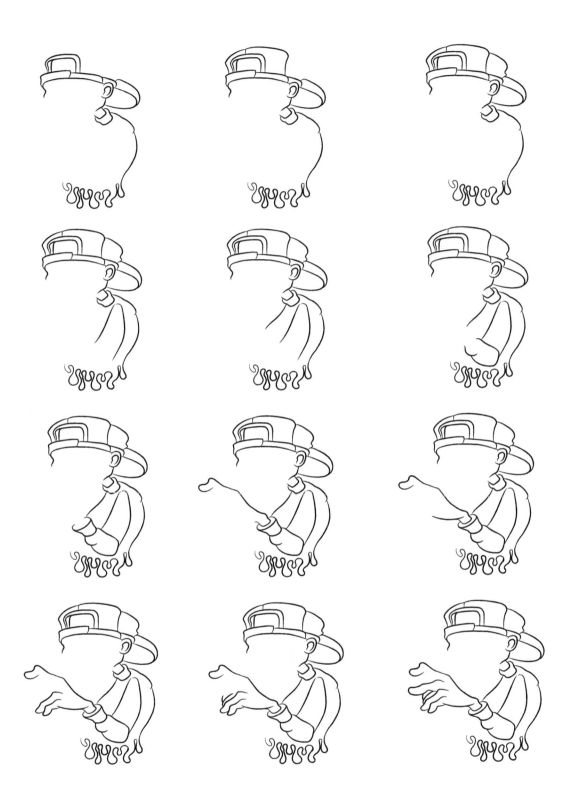

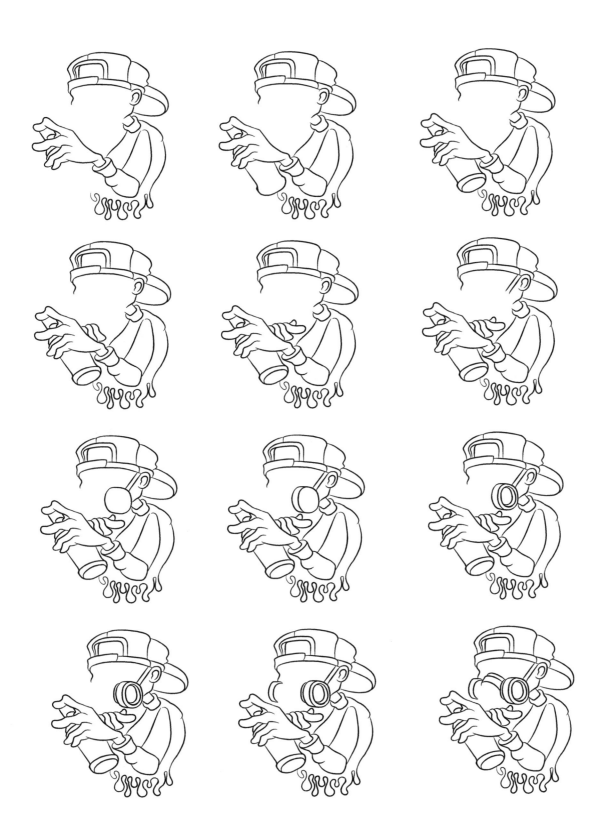

You can download blank grids to practice with in dark and light PDF formats by following the link below.

https://www.lipdf.com/product/grids/

28. You can make your drawing more
original by exaggerating some of its features.

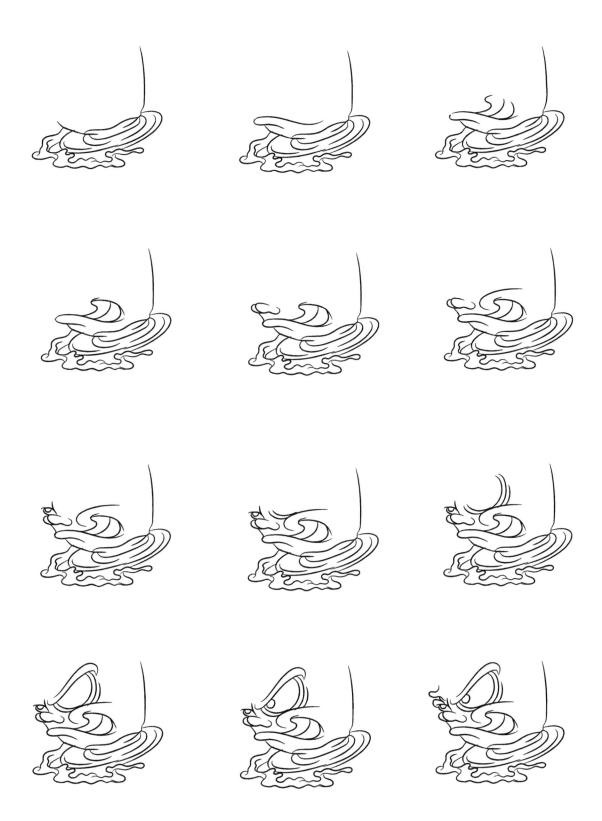

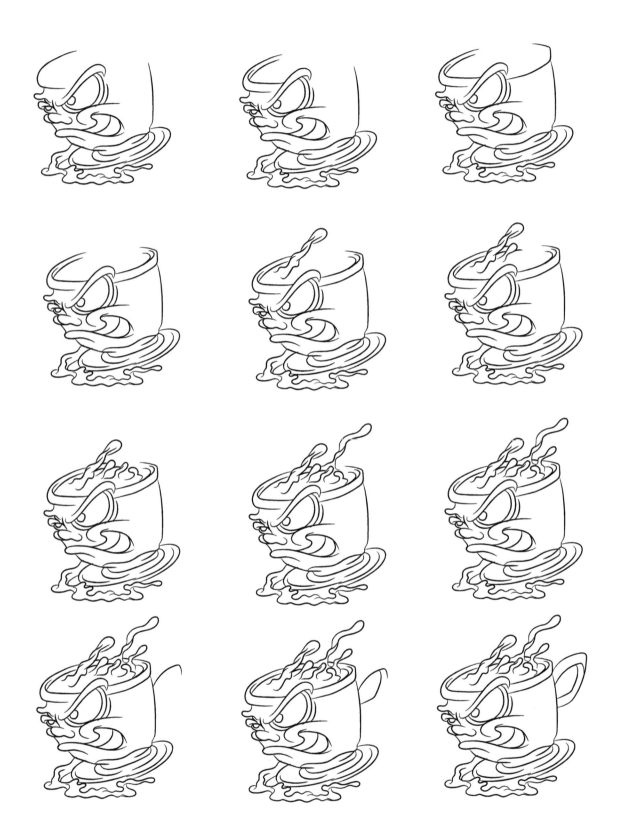

You can download blank grids to practice with in dark and light PDF formats by following the link below.

https://www.lipdf.com/product/grids/

29. Try out doodling on a scrap piece of paper before starting this drawing, it will help with your concentration and creativity!

You can download blank grids to practice with in dark and light PDF formats by following the link below.

https://www.lipdf.com/product/grids/

30. Try enlarging different parts of your drawings to create different effects.

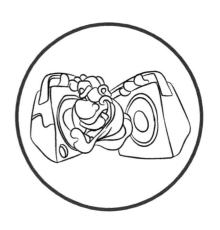

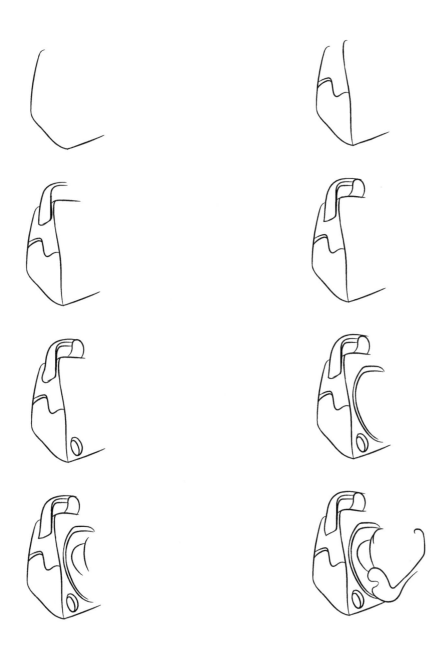

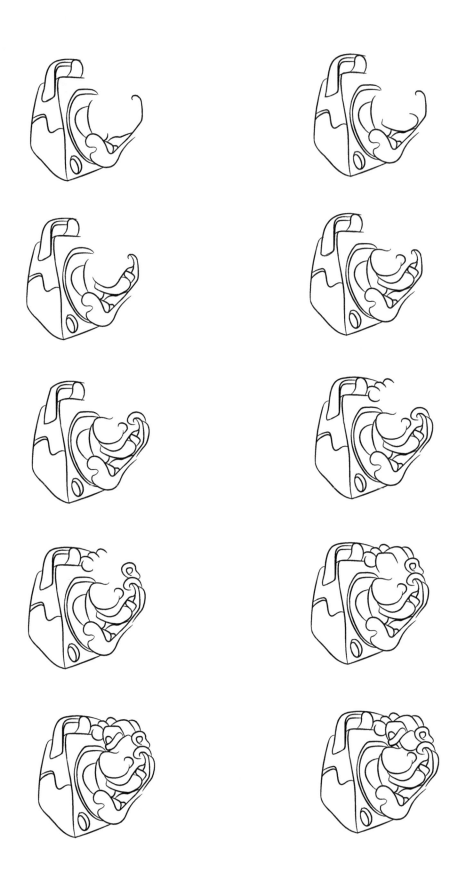

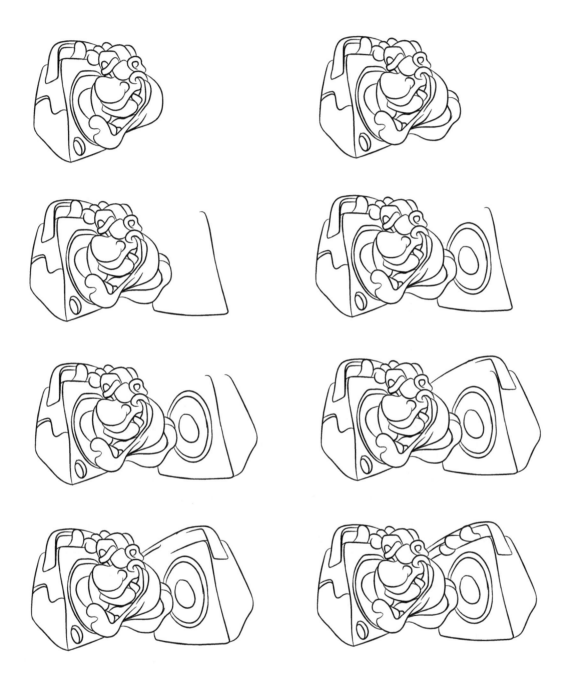

You can download blank grids to practice with in dark and light PDF formats by following the link below.

https://www.lipdf.com/product/grids/

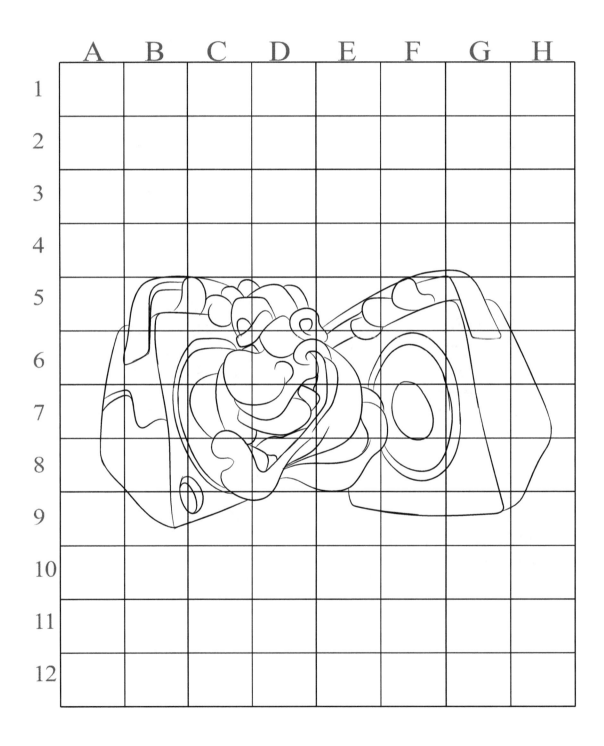

CPSIA information can be obtained
at www.ICGtesting.com
Printed in the USA
LVHW060550150122
708488LV00007B/136